WORD PROBLEMS
4TH GRADE
Digital Mathematics
Children's Math Books

SPEEDY
PUBLISHING

Speedy Publishing LLC
40 E. Main St. #1156
Newark, DE 19711
www.speedypublishing.com

Read and answer each question.
Put your solution and answer
on the space provided.

1 Karen had 2,065 Legos, but she lost 18 Legos. How many Legos does she have now?

2 Luke baked 115 muffins. John baked 12 times as many. How many muffins did John bake?

3 Joseph has 6 boxes of pencils. If each box of pencil holds 7 pencils, how many pencils does Joseph have?

4 Sam put 84 books in to 12 boxes. If each box held an equal amount, how many books were in each?

5 There are 24 erasers and 12 students. If the erasers were divided up equally, how many would each student get?

6 Drew collected 32 oranges. If he shared them among 8 friends, how many did he give each friend?

7 Julie gave away an equal amount of flowers to each of her 3 friends. If she had 42 flowers, how many did she give each friend?

8 Andy has 10,000 balloons. 784 of them are red and the rest are green. How many green balloons does Andy have?

9 There are 14,240 books in a library. They are arranged on shelves that hold 8 books each. How many shelves are in the library?

10 At a birthday party you counted 60 eyes. How many people were at the party?

11 There are 3 dozen cats that need to be adopted. There are 2 dozen dogs that need to adopted. How many dogs and cats need to be adopted in all?

12 Casey read 21 pages of her book every day, for 7 days in a row. How many pages did Casey read?

13 The maximum capacity of a concert hall is 3,500. There are 2,674 people in the hall now. How many more people are able to see the concert before it reaches capacity?

14 There are 5 black cats and 6 white cats. The black cats each weigh 12 pounds. The white cats each weigh 15 pounds. How much do they weigh altogether?

15 A clown came to the party with 40 blue balloons and 65 white balloons. Half of the blue balloons popped and 10 of the white balloons flew away. How many did the clown have left to give away to the kids?

16 Mario has 4 packages of gum. There are 16 pieces in each package. How many pieces of gum does Mario have?

17 Maggi had 2 packages of cupcakes. There are 5 cupcakes in each package. She ate 4 cupcakes. How many are left?

18 21 people are going to the zoo. There are 3 vans to take people to the zoo. How many will go in each van if the same number go in each van and all of the people go to the zoo?

19 I counted all the pockets I had on my clothes today. Altogether I had twenty-six pockets. I had seven on my shirt and thirteen on my pants. How many pockets were on my jacket?

20 Vincent is 14 years old. His grandmother is 6 times as old as he is. How old is Vincent's grandmother?

21 Joel was walking in the park and saw a flock of 2,362 birds flying. How many total wings were in the flock?

22 Janice had 1,109 dolls and Hazel had 2,136 dolls. If they put their dolls together, how many would they have?

23 My dog had some bones. Then, he dug up 248 bones. Now he has 670 bones. How many bones did he start with?

24 George scored 156 goals playing soccer last season. This season he scored 187 goals. What is the total number of goals George scored?

25 Henry needs to read a 624 page book for school. He has already read 135 pages. How many pages does he have left to read?

26 Wesley made 92 baskets on Sunday. He made 161 baskets on Monday. How many baskets did he make in all?

27 Michelle picked 341 apples.

Phil ate 176 of the apples.

How many apples are left?

28 Angel bought 850 pieces of paper. She used 223 pieces of the paper. How many pieces of paper does she have left?

29 Mr. Bill impressed 2,325 fans at the basketball game on Friday. If the fans were seated in equal groups on 3 sets of bleachers, how many fans were on each set?

30 Mrs. Marcus bought 4 pizzas with 8 slices each. She and her friends ate 21 slices of the pizza. How many slices were left?

31 Mrs. Gil gave $0.50 to each fourth grader. If there are 69 fourth graders, how much money did Mrs. Hilt give away?

32 Mr. Thompson looked at his car's odometer before a trip. The odometer showed that he had traveled 211.3 miles. When he stopped for lunch, the odometer read 382.0. How many miles had he traveled?

ANSWERS

1. Karen had 2,065 Legos, but she lost 18 Legos. How many Legos does she have now?
2065 - 18 = 2047

2. Luke baked 115 muffins. John baked 12 times as many. How many muffins did John bake?
115 x 12 = 1380

3. Joseph has 6 boxes of pencils. If each box of pencil holds 7 pencils, how many pencils does Joseph have?
6 x 7 = 42

4. Sam put 84 books in to 12 boxes. If each box held an equal amount, how many books were in each?
84 ÷ 12 = 7

5. There are 24 erasers and 12 students. If the erasers were divided up equally, how many would each student get?
24 ÷ 12 = 2

6. Drew collected 32 oranges. If he shared them among 8 friends, how many did he give each friend?
32 ÷ 8 = 4

7. Julie gave away an equal amount of flowers to each of her 3 friends. If she had 42 flowers, how many did she give each friend?
42 ÷ 3 = 14

8. Andy has 10,000 balloons. 784 of them are red and the rest are green. How many green balloons does Andy have?
10000 - 784 = 9216

9. There are 14,240 books in a library. They are arranged on shelves that hold 8 books each. How many shelves are in the library?
14240 ÷ 8 = 1780

10   At a birthday party you counted 60 eyes. How many people were at the party?

60 ÷ 2 = 30

11   There are 3 dozen cats that need to be adopted. There are 2 dozen dogs that need to adopted. How many dogs and cats need to be adopted in all?

12 x 3 = 36   12 x 2 = 24

36 + 24 = 60

12   Casey read 21 pages of her book every day, for 7 days in a row. How many pages did Casey read?

21 x 7 = 147

13   The maximum capacity of a concert hall is 3,500. There are 2,674 people in the hall now. How many more people are able to see the concert before it reaches capacity?

3500 - 2674 = 826

14   There are 5 black cats and 6 white cats. The black cats each weigh 12 pounds. The white cats each weigh 15 pounds. How much do they weigh altogether?

5 x 12 = 60   6 x 15 = 90

60 + 90 = 150

15   A clown came to the party with 40 blue balloons and 65 white balloons. Half of the blue balloons popped and 10 of the white balloons flew away. How many did the clown have left to give away to the kids?

40 ÷ 2 = 20   65 - 10 = 55

20 + 55 = 75

16   Mario has 4 packages of gum. There are 16 pieces in each package. How many pieces of gum does Mario have?

4 x 16 = 64

17   Maggi had 2 packages of cupcakes. There are 5 cupcakes in each package. She ate 4 cupcakes. How many are left?

2 x 5 = 10 - 4 = 6

18   21 people are going to the zoo. There are 3 vans to take people to the zoo. How many will go in each van if the same number go in each van and all of the people go to the zoo?
21 ÷ 3 = 7

19   I counted all the pockets I had on my clothes today. Altogether I had twenty-six pockets. I had seven on my shirt and thirteen on my pants. How many pockets were on my jacket?
26 - 7 - 13 = 6

20   Vincent is 14 years old. His grandmother is 6 times as old as he is. How old is Vincent's grandmother?
14 x 6 = 84

21   Joel was walking in the park and saw a flock of 2,362 birds flying. How many total wings were in the flock?
2362 x 2 = 4724

22   Janice had 1,109 dolls and Hazel had 2,136 dolls. If they put their dolls together, how many would they have?
1109 + 2136 = 3245

23   My dog had some bones. Then, he dug up 248 bones. Now he has 670 bones. How many bones did he start with?
670 - 248 = 422

24   George scored 156 goals playing soccer last season. This season he scored 187 goals. What is the total number of goals George scored?
156 + 187 = 343

25   Henry needs to read a 624 page book for school. He has already read 135 pages. How many pages does he have left to read?
624 - 135 = 489

26 Wesley made 92 baskets on Sunday. He made 161 baskets on Monday. How many baskets did he make in all?
92 + 161 = 253

27 Michelle picked 341 apples. Phil ate 176 of the apples. How many apples are left?
341 - 176 = 165

28 Angel bought 850 pieces of paper. She used 223 pieces of the paper. How many pieces of paper does she have left?
850 - 223 = 627

29 Mr. Bill impressed 2,325 fans at the basketball game on Friday. If the fans were seated in equal groups on 3 sets of bleachers, how many fans were on each set?
2325 ÷3 = 775

30 Mrs. Marcus bought 4 pizzas with 8 slices each. She and her friends ate 21 slices of the pizza. How many slices were left?
4 x 8 = 32 - 21 = 11

31 Mrs. Gil gave $0.50 to each fourth grader. If there are 69 fourth graders, how much money did Mrs. Hilt give away?
69 x .5 = 34.5

32 Mr. Thompson looked at his car's odometer before a trip. The odometer showed that he had traveled 211.3 miles. When he stopped for lunch, the odometer read 382.0. How many miles had he traveled?
382.0 - 211.3 = 170.7

Made in the USA
Las Vegas, NV
31 October 2021